HEALTHY BODY
Safety

Text by Carol Ballard • Photography by Robert Pickett

BLACKBIRCH®
PRESS

THOMSON
™
GALE

San Diego • Detroit • New York • San Francisco • Cleveland • New Haven, Conn. • Waterville, Maine • London • Munich

TITLES IN THE HEALTHY BODY SERIES:

• Personal Hygiene • Eating Right • Safety • Exercise • Relationships • Harmful Substances

© 2004 by White-Thompson Publishing Ltd.

Produced by White-Thompson Publishing Ltd.
2/3 St. Andrew's Place
Lewes BN7 1UP, U.K.

For more information, contact
The Gale Group
27500 Drake Rd.
Farmington Hills, MI 48331-3535
Or you can visit our Internet site at http://www.gale.com

Editor:	Elaine Fuoco-Lang
Consultant:	Chris Sculthorpe, East Sussex, Brighton & Hove Healthy School Scheme Co-ordinator
Inside design:	Joelle Wheelwright
Cover design:	Hodder Wayland
Photographs:	Robert Pickett
Proofreader:	Jane Colgan
Artwork:	Peter Bull

Acknowledgements:

The publishers would like to thank the following for their assistance with this book: the staff and children at Drapers Mills Primary School, Margate, Kent.

Originally published by Hodder Wayland, an imprint of Hodder Children's Books, a division of Hodder Headline Limited 338 Euston Road, London NW1 3BH

Picture acknowledgements:
Tim Pannell/Corbis 5 bottom, Yang Liu/Corbis 6, Mug Shots/Corbis 10, Ronnie Kaufman/Corbis 11 top, Progressive Image/Corbis 12 bottom, Daniel Mirer/Corbis 17 bottom, George Hall/Corbis 23 bottom, Firefly Productions/Corbis 24, Corbis 25, David Butow/Corbis SABA 29 right; Angela Hampton 14, 16, 19 top, 21; Hodder Wayland Picture Library 8, 9 top, 11 bottom; Robert Pickett 9 bottom, 12 top, 13, 15, 17 top, 18, 19 bottom, 20, 23 top, 26, 27, 28, 29 left; WTPix 4, 22.
The photographs in this book are of models who have granted their permission for their use in this title.

LIBRARY OF CONGRESS CATALOGING-IN-PUBLICATION DATA

Ballard, Carol.
    Safety / by Carol Ballard.
    v. cm. — (Healthy body)
Includes bibliographical references and index.
Contents: Safety matters—At home—Play safe!—Out and about—On the sidewalk—On the road—At the pool—At the beach—Computers and communications—Fire!—Safe celebrations—First aid—Emergency!
    ISBN 1-4103-0156-7 (hardback : alk. paper)
    1. Safety education—Junvenile literature. 2. Accidents—Prevention—Juvenile literature. 3. Children's accidents—Prevention—Juvenile literature. [1. Safety. 2. Accidents—Prevention.] I. Title. II. Series.
    HQ770.7.B34 2004
    613.6—dc22

                                        2003012015

Printed in China
10 9 8 7 6 5 4 3 2 1

Contents

Safety matters

Wherever you are, whatever you do, it is important to be careful. Adults can help you to be safe. They cannot do everything, though. You have a big role to play, too. You can learn what it is safe to do, where it is safe to go, and who it is safe to be with. This knowledge can help keep you and the people around you from harm.

▼ *Wearing protective clothing can help prevent injuries when you play sports.*

This book tells you about some of the ways in which you can stay safe at home and when you go out to play. It gives you some suggestions for keeping safe on the streets and other places such as swimming pools and beaches. You will find guidance about first aid for yourself and other people. You will also learn about what to do in an emergency.

▲ *Signs like this warn about dangers around you.*

There are many things you can do to be responsible for your own safety. Make sure you always listen to and follow advice from adults you can trust, such as parents and teachers.

▶ *Take care when playing with your friends.*

At home

We all like to think of our homes as being safe places, but accidents can happen all too easily. Many accidents are the result of people being careless or lazy.

Kitchens contain many things that, if not used properly, could be dangerous. Sharp knives, stoves, and cleaning materials all need to be used very carefully.

Many of the things we use every day need electricity. Follow these safety rules when using electrical appliances:

● Never touch anything electrical with wet hands.

● Never poke a socket or appliance with anything.

● Never take anything electrical apart.

● Always switch electrical appliances OFF when they are not being used.

● If you spot an old, frayed wire, tell an adult.

▲ *Microwave ovens, toasters, and stoves can all be dangerous if they are not used correctly.*

Being untidy is the cause of many accidents! People can easily trip over toys and other things that are left lying around. Make sure you put things away when you have finished with them.

It is a long way to fall from the top of the stairs to the bottom! It makes sense not to play on or around stairs or outdoor steps.

▲ *DANGER! This symbol shows us that we should take care.*

Action Zone

Toddlers and young children are particularly at risk from harmful substances like cleaning materials. They do not yet know what is safe to eat and drink and what is not. Cleaning materials should always be kept in their original containers. Do not use them unless an adult has told you to. Always read the safety warnings on the label. You can help keep younger brothers and sisters safe by keeping things like cleaning materials out of their reach. If your cupboards have childproof latches, make sure they are fastened.

▲ *Household chemicals, such as bleach, may have these symbols on them. They warn that the product can be poisonous (left) and corrosive (right).*

Play safe!

Playing is fun—and you can make sure that your games are safe for you and the people you are playing with.

If you are playing with younger children, think about their safety as well as your own. Do not let them play with toys or games that have small pieces. They often put little things in their mouths and can easily choke. Remember they are smaller than you, so try not to play rough games in which they might fall down or get hurt.

▲ *Older children can help keep younger ones safe.*

Toys and games

Toys and games that need batteries should be looked after carefully. When the battery runs down, ask an adult to help you change it. If a battery has leaked, ask an adult to make the toy safe.

When you have finished playing with a toy or game, make sure you put it away properly, so that nobody will trip over it. This is good for everybody in your house—and it is good for your game, too!

Where to play

Try to choose a sensible place to play. A yard is a good place for a running game. A landing or staircase is not because you could easily fall downstairs. If you want to go to a park or playground, always ask an adult first. Make sure you tell him or her where you are going, who you will be with, and when you will be back. Once you have done that, make sure you stick to what you have said—do not decide to go somewhere else instead.

◄ *When you play outside, make sure an adult knows where you are.*

⁀ Action Zone

Are all your toys safe to play with? Go and check them. Pick up each toy one at a time and look carefully at it. Is it broken? Does it have any sharp edges? Could it hurt you or a younger child in any way? If the answer to any of these questions is "yes," ask an adult to make the toy safe.

▶ *Broken toys can be very dangerous. Make sure you let an adult know if one of your toys is broken. The broken windshield on this car has left sharp edges that should only be handled by an adult.*

Out and about

It is fun to go out to play or to be with your friends. Think about how you can keep yourself safe.

Some places are safer than others. Unless you are with an adult, avoid playing in woods and sheltered spots. Open parks and playgrounds are much better, because there are people all around. Try not to play near water because there is always a danger of falling in. Frozen ponds and streams are pretty, but never be tempted to try to walk on them. The ice may be thinner than you expect and can break under your weight.

▲ **When you are out playing, remember to keep safe.**

Out on your own

It is a good idea to stay with at least one other person instead of going off on your own. You can help each other if there is a problem. Although it makes sense never to talk to strangers, you might need some help if you get separated from the people you are with. In a store or shopping center, there will usually be an official person around for you to talk to. If not, look for an adult with his or her own family. Ask that person to help you.

▲ *If you are out in cold weather, wearing layers of clothing will help you stay warm.*

Clothing

Wherever you go, make sure you wear the right clothing. If it is a cold day, wrap up well. Several layers of clothes will keep you warmer than one thick layer. A waterproof layer is a good idea too, in case it starts to rain. If you are going to be out when it gets dark, make sure you can be seen by motorists and other people. Reflective strips on your clothes show up in bright car headlights and help to make you stand out in the dark. Carrying a flashlight is also a good idea, so you can see and be seen.

 # Healthy Hints

Feet are important—and so are the things that you wear on them! Think carefully about what you are going to be doing and choose footwear that matches the activity. For example, hiking boots are good for walking over rough ground. Rubber-soled sneakers are good for sports that require running.

▲ *Be sure to wear the right footwear for the activity you are doing.*

On the sidewalk

Walking on the sidewalk is usually safe—but do you know how to cross a street safely?

First, find a safe place to cross. If there is a pedestrian crossing nearby, use it. If not, find a place where the road is straight and you can see clearly in both directions. Stand at the edge of the sidewalk. Look first in the direction the traffic is coming from on your side of the road—usually to your left. If there is nothing, look the other way— usually to your right. If there is nothing coming, look in the first direction again. If that is still clear, walk quickly and sensibly across the road.

▲ *Be careful when crossing the street.*

If you use a pedestrian crossing with lights, press the button and wait for the signal that tells you it is safe to cross. At many crossings, an upraised red hand changes to a white or green walking person when it is safe to cross. At other crossings, a sign may simply say "walk."

◄ *A crossing guard can help you cross the street safely.*

Never be tempted to cross a road from behind a vehicle such as an ice cream truck. You will be hidden by the vehicle, so a car driver may not see you until it is too late. You could be badly hurt.

Action Zone

Find a map of your neighborhood that shows your street, school, park, and anywhere else you go regularly. If you cannot find a map, draw a simple one and mark important places and streets on it. Can you find a safe route to each place? Where are the safe places to cross the roads? Do you know where the pedestrian crossings are?

Playing ball on a sidewalk or in the street is dangerous. If you do play on a sidewalk, never run into the road to get your ball back. You could easily be hit by a car or other vehicle.

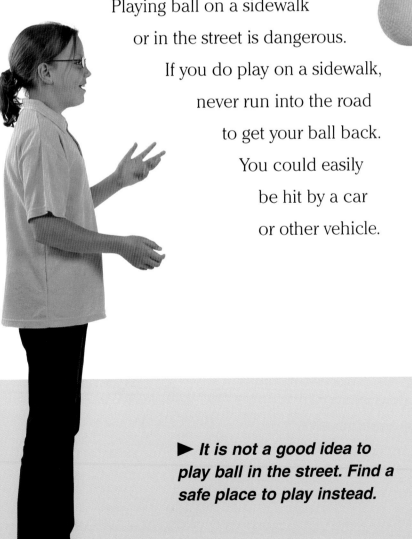

▶ *It is not a good idea to play ball in the street. Find a safe place to play instead.*

On the road

Cars, buses, and bicycles can be dangerous. You can help stay safe by following a few simple precautions.

Motor vehicles

When you ride in a car, always put your seat belt on. On a bus, do not stand up or move around while the vehicle is in motion. Whether you are in a car or on a bus, never distract the driver. He or she needs to concentrate on driving.

Bicycles

Make sure you can ride your bike confidently and safely before you ride it in the street. Know what common road signs mean and know how to signal when you are turning right or left. Remember to stop and look both ways before you ride out into the street, just as you would if you were going to cross the street on foot.

▶ *Wearing a seat belt is the law and helps protect you if you have an accident.*

Ride on the correct side of the road and obey all road signs and traffic signals. Check behind you before you turn or change lanes. If you are bicycling with other people, do not ride more than two side by side. On narrow or busy roads always ride one behind the other. Remember it is dangerous to hold onto another bicyclist or carry a passenger on your bike.

▶ *Wear a helmet and reflective clothing when you ride your bike.*

 # Healthy Hints

Follow these guidelines to make sure your bike is safe to ride.

● Make sure your bike is the right size for you. Without bending your legs, you should be able to put both feet on the ground when sitting on the seat.

● Check that the brakes work properly and the tires are pumped up. The chain should be oiled and adjusted properly.

● Do not put a bag on the handlebars to carry things. This makes it hard to keep your balance, and it could get caught in the front wheel.

● Wear a helmet and reflective clothing.

● If you will be out in the dark, make sure your front and back lights work properly.

▲ *Be sure your bike is in good shape before you ride it in the street.*

At the pool

Swimming pools are great places to have fun! But having fun does not mean forgetting how to stay safe.

Do not swim unless there is an adult watching. Most swimming pools have a lifeguard on duty. This person often sits on a raised platform so he or she can see everything that is happening. If you have a problem, try to attract the lifeguard's attention by shouting or waving your arms.

▲ *If you are not a very experienced swimmer, make sure an adult is watching you.*

Unless you are a strong swimmer, stay in the shallow end of the pool. Make sure you can stand up. If you cannot put your feet on the bottom of the pool, go back to shallower water. Usually the depth is marked on the wall of the pool. This lets you check how deep the water is where you are.

▲ When you are learning to swim, a float helps you to gain confidence in the water.

Think about other pool users. Try not to splash other people, and never try to hold somebody under the water. If you want to dive in, go to the deep end of the pool. If you want to jump in, make sure nobody else is in the area. Obey the rules of the pool. Use balls, floats, and other equipment only when and where it is allowed.

The area around the pool is often wet and slippery, so always walk around rather than running.

 # Healthy Hints

One of the good things about swimming in a swimming pool is that the water is clean and safe. The water in the pool is being changed all the time. Before clean water flows into the pool, chemicals are added to kill any germs. A constant stream of dirty water flows out of the pool. You can play your part in keeping the pool clean for yourself and other swimmers to enjoy. Remember to go to the bathroom before you swim. Avoid wearing outdoor shoes when you are in the pool surroundings. Never drop trash into or around the pool.

▲ Lifeguards make sure that people are safe in the water.

At the beach

Many people have wonderful vacations at the beach. Beaches can be dangerous, though, unless you follow a few simple guidelines.

Always check that the beach is safe for swimming, and do not go into the water without permission. Be aware that the bottom can suddenly dip down. The water can quickly get much deeper than you expect.

► *Inflatables should not be used where there are waves and currents.*

Strong currents can be dangerous and pull you away from the beach. Many beaches have special safety flags. These flags show areas where it is safe to swim and other areas where it is more dangerous. Look for the flags and stay within the safe areas. Inflatables can be fun, but should not be used in the sea. They can get swept out into deep water by the waves and current.

◄ *Tide pools are home to different animals. Make sure that you are careful near them. Even shallow water can be dangerous.*

Cliffs and caves

It can be tempting to explore cliffs and caves, but there may be hidden dangers. Do not climb cliffs unless an adult is with you. Do not go into caves alone. Before you play at the foot of cliffs, check there is not a sign warning of falling rocks.

Rocks on beaches are good for climbing on, but remember that seaweed and water can make them very slippery. Be careful where you put your feet. Walk carefully and do not run.

▲ *Being aware of dangers can make your trip to the beach a safe one.*

Action Zone

Nobody likes to play or sunbathe on a dirty beach. Try to make sure that you leave the beach as clean and tidy as you can. Put all your litter in a trash can or take it home with you. Cans may have sharp edges that can cause a nasty cut. Glass is dangerous too because it can easily be broken.

▲ *Try to avoid taking cans and glass to the beach. Choose things to eat and drink that come in plastic containers instead.*

Computers & communications

Computers and cell phones make communications easy. There are some, though, that you should avoid.

Cell phones

Cell phones are a great way to stay in touch with your friends and family. Some scientists, however, think that using a cell phone for long periods may lead to health problems. A hands-free set may help reduce this risk, because you do not need to hold the phone to your head when you use it.

► *Using a cell phone for long periods is not a good idea.*

Computers

Many families have computers and are connected to the Internet. Some people think it is better to have the computer in a room that the whole family uses, rather than in a bedroom. That way, other people might spot a problem you have not noticed. You are also not shutting yourself away from the rest of the family.

◄ *When you use a computer, be sure to take a break now and then.*

Chat rooms

Chat rooms are fun, but you need to take care. Always tell an adult what you are doing, and who you are chatting with. Never give your name, home address, school address, or telephone number to someone in a chat room. Never arrange to meet somebody you have met in a chat room. You have no way of knowing if they are pretending to be someone very different from who they really are.

Sometimes you may feel upset or worried by something you find on the Internet, or by something that is said in a chat room. If this happens, tell an adult so they can sort it out for you and keep it from happening again.

Games

Some people who play computer games a lot can actually become addicted to them. This can cause all sorts of problems, and can take a long time to get over. Try to limit the length of time you spend using your computer. Make sure you get plenty of active fun as well.

Healthy Hints

Your body was not designed to sit in one place for hours on end staring at a little screen! Be kind to your body. Give it a break now and then by getting up and moving around a bit. Your eyes will get tired if they stare at the screen too much, so try not to use the computer for very long periods of time. Try to sit straight too, so that your back does not get stiff and bunched up.

▲ *Playing computer games is fine, but you should play active games, too.*

Fire!

We have all heard the wailing of fire engine sirens as they rush to tackle a blaze somewhere. Know what to do in case of a fire.

One of the first signs of fire is usually smoke. A smoke alarm can detect smoke long before people can, and makes a loud noise so you know there is danger.

If you hear a smoke alarm going off, make your way out of the building. Try to stay calm.

▲ *A fire engine goes into action.*

Preventing fires

If a fire does start, do not try to put it out on your own. Get out of the building. Call the fire department. Do not go back into the building for any reason at all, however important it may seem to you.

You can help to prevent fires from starting. Do not play with matches or cigarette lighters, throw things onto open fires, or play near heaters.

It can be all too easy to start fires outdoors, too. Matches are just as dangerous outside as they are inside. In dry weather, grass and other plants can easily catch fire, and the flames may spread very quickly. Never try to light a bonfire outside without an adult to help you.

▲ *Remember that candles, matches, and lighters are not toys.*

Action Zone

It is very unlikely that there will ever be a fire at your home. Just in case, though, you should know exactly how you would get to safety. Draw a floor plan of your home, marking stairs, hallways, doors, and windows. Each room should have two different exit routes, in case one is blocked. Talk to the rest of your family and check that you all have your escape routes planned. Make sure you can get out of windows if necessary. Choose a safe place outside where the family can meet once you have escaped from the building.

▲ *Know how to get out of your house in case of fire.*

Safe celebrations

Bonfires and fireworks are part of many celebrations. Most public displays are carefully organized so that everything is as safe as possible. If you have fireworks at home, remember that they are dangerous so you must be careful with them. Follow these precautions:

▲ *It is best to watch fireworks from a safe distance.*

● All fireworks should be handled by an adult. Children should not touch them.

● Store fireworks in a metal box and only take out one at a time. Never put fireworks in a pocket.

● Carefully follow the instructions on each firework.

- Stand well away from fireworks because sparks can travel long distances.
- Never go back to a firework that has been lit.
- Never throw fireworks.
- Keep pets indoors.

People often light candles at times of celebration. Candles should always stand on a heatproof base. Keep them well away from anything that could dangle into the flame. They should never be left alight in a room when nobody is there.

Electric lights are also used during celebrations. Before they are plugged in, an adult should check that the wires are safe.

▶ **Candles are lit to celebrate Kwanzaa, the African American holiday.**

Fantastic Facts

The first fireworks were made in China. The color of a firework depends on the type of metal it contains. Different metals burn with different colors. Strontium gives red sparks. Copper gives blue sparks. Barium gives green sparks, and magnesium gives bright silvery white sparks.

First aid

We all hurt ourselves from time to time. You can treat some minor injuries yourself. More serious accidents, though, will need to be treated by an adult and sometimes by a doctor. If you do not know what to do, always ask an adult for help.

To treat a small cut or scrape, clean the skin thoroughly with water and antiseptic. Sometimes you may need to cover it with a bandage.

► *If you cut yourself, be sure to carefully clean the area with an antiseptic wipe.*

▼ *A wasp should not sting you unless you annoy it.*

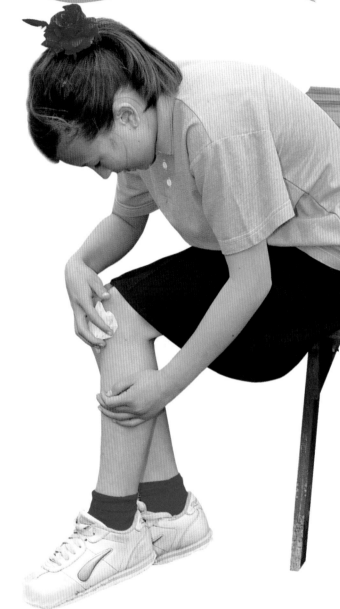

Insect stings and bites can hurt a lot! Some creams and sprays can take away the stinging feeling, but always check with an adult before you use them.

If you fall and it hurts to move, stay where you are. Get a friend to go for help. If a friend falls and cannot move without a lot of pain, do not try to move them. Go get help as quickly as you can.

A burn or scald needs immediate action to take the heat away from the skin. If you can, run cold water over the skin until it stops hurting quite so much. Never put anything on burned skin. Always ask an adult for help as soon as you can.

◄ *If you are hurt, ask a friend for help.*

 # Healthy Hints

Your skin is your body's outer protective layer. It prevents dirt and germs from getting inside your body. When you cut yourself, your skin is broken, so it is easy for germs to get inside. You must clean a cut or scrape thoroughly to prevent this from happening. Washing with lots of water will flush any dirt away from the cut. An antiseptic wipe or spray will kill any germs that remain. Covering the cut with a bandage will help keep it clean while the skin heals.

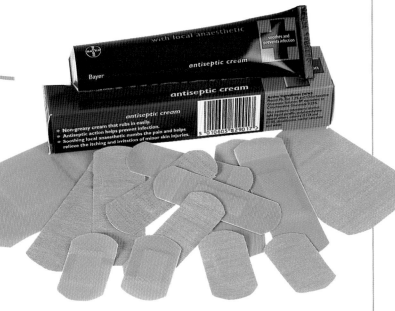

▲ *Bandages and creams may be used on minor cuts or scrapes.*

Emergency!

▼ Dial 911 in an emergency.

We all hope we never have to deal with an emergency. It is a good idea to know what to do, though, just in case.

- When you need help quickly, go to the nearest telephone. You can use a cell phone or a pay phone. Emergency calls are free, so you can make one even if you have no money.

- If you are using a pay phone, lift the receiver and dial 911, the emergency number.

- When the operator answers, he or she will ask you which service you need. You need to say whether you need the police, the fire department, or an ambulance.

● Stay as calm as you can. Listen to the questions the operator asks and answer them carefully. He or she will need to know where you are, what has happened, and who is in trouble. Sometimes, he or she may ask you to do something.

● Make sure you listen carefully and follow instructions exactly. If you do not understand, ask the operator to repeat the instructions.

● The emergency service you have asked for will soon be on its way to help you.

 Fantastic Facts

Some people think it is funny to make "hoax" calls. This means making an untrue call to an emergency service. The emergency services may then be tied up investigating a hoax call when they are needed somewhere else in a true emergency. Other people damage pay phones deliberately. This means that people cannot contact emergency services when they need to. Never be tempted to do either of these things. You could be keeping emergency services from saving somebody's life.

▲ *Remember to stay calm if you make an emergency call. Give the operator as much information as you can.*

Glossary

addicted become so used to something that you cannot do without it.

antiseptic lotion, cream, liquid, or spray that kills germs.

childproof something designed so that a child cannot operate it.

corrosive a substance that will eat into the skin and other materials.

current strong pull by water in one direction.

germ a tiny living thing that can cause illness.

heatproof does not let heat through and is not damaged by heat.

illuminated lit up so that it is easy to see.

inflatable can be blown up by air, like a balloon.

pedestrian a person who is walking.

precaution something done to prevent an accident from happening.

reflective shines when a light shines on it.

waterproof does not let water through and is not damaged by water.

For more information

Boelts, Maribeth, *Kid's Guide to Staying Safe Around Fire*. NY Rosen, 2003.

Mattern, Joanne, *Safety at Home*. ABDO, 1999.

McGregor, Cynthia, *Ten Steps to Staying Safe*. NY: Rosen, 2003.

Raatma, Lucia, *Safety at the Swimming Pool*. Mankato, MN: Capstone Press, 2000.

———, *Safety on Your Bicycle*. Mankato, MN: Capstone Press, 2000.

Index